The Gold Standard in Books for Your Board

Read each in an hour • Mix & match for bulk discounts up to 45 percent

Fund Raising Realities Every Board Member Must Face
Revised Ed., David Lansdowne, 112 pp., $24.95, ISBN 1889102326

Over 100,000 board members and development officers across America have used this book to help them raise substantial money – in sluggish and robust economies. Have your board spend just *one* hour with this classic and they'll come to understand virtually everything they need to know about raising big gifts. Among the bestselling fundraising books of all time.

Asking Jerold Panas, 112 pp., $24.95, ISBN 1889102172

It ranks right up there with public speaking. Nearly all of us fear it. And yet it's critical to our success. *Asking for money*. What this book convincingly shows is that nearly everyone, regardless of their persuasive ability, can become an effective fundraiser if they follow Jerold Panas' step-by-step guidelines.

The Ultimate Board Member's Book
Revised Ed., Kay Sprinkel Grace, 114 pp., $24.95, ISBN 1889102393

Here is a book for *all* nonprofit boards:
• Those wanting to operate at peak efficiency,
• Those needing to clarify exactly what their job is, and,
• Those wanting to ensure that all members - novice and veteran - are "on the same page" with respect to roles and responsibilities.

It's all here in jargon-free language: what the job entails, fundraising responsibilities, conflicts of interest, effective recruiting, and more.

How Are We Doing?
Gayle L. Gifford, 120 pp., $24.95, ISBN 1889102237

Until now, almost all books dealing with board evaluation have had an air of unreality about them. The perplexing graphs, the matrix boxes, the overlong questionnaires. Enter Gayle Gifford, who has pioneered an elegantly simple way for your board to evaluate and improve its overall performance. It all comes down to answering a host of simple, straightforward questions.

The 11 Questions Every Donor Asks
Harvey McKinnon, 108 pp., $24.95, ISBN 1889102377

A watershed book, *The 11 Questions* prepares you for the tough questions you'll inevitably face from prospective donors. Harvey McKinnon identifies 11 such questions, ranging from "Why me?" to "Will my gift make a difference?" to "Will I have a say over how you use my gift?" And the suggested answers are illuminating and will largely dictate your fundraising success.

Emerson & Church, Publishers
www.emersonandchurch.com

BIG GIFTS FOR SMALL GROUPS

A Board Member's 1-Hour Guide
to Securing Gifts of $500 to $5,000

First printed September 2004

10 9 8 7 6 5 4

Printed in the United States of America
This text is printed on acid-free paper.

Copies of this book are available from the publisher at discount when purchased in quantity for boards of directors or staff.

Emerson & Church, Publishers
P.O. Box 338 • Medfield, MA 02052
Tel. 508-359-0019 • Fax 508-359-2703
www.emersonandchurch.com

Library of Congress Cataloging-in-Publication Data

Robinson, Andy.
  Big gifts for small groups : a 1-hour board member's guide to securing gifts of $500 to $5,000 / Andy Robinson.
      p. cm.
  ISBN 1-889102-21-0 (pbk. : alk. paper)
  1. Fund raising. 2. Charities--Finance. I. Title.
  HV41.2.R63 2004
    361.7'632'0681--dc22

                                                          2004015842

ANDY ROBINSON

BIG GIFTS
for
SMALL GROUPS

A Board Member's 1-Hour Guide
to Securing Gifts of $500 to $5,000

Emerson
& Church
PUBLISHERS

COMPANION BOOK BY ANDY ROBINSON

Yours is a good board, but you want it to be better. You want:

- Clearly defined objectives
- Meetings with more focus
- Broader participation in fundraising
- And more follow-through between meetings.

You want these and a dozen other tangibles and intangibles that will propel your board from good to great.

Say hello to your guide, Andy Robinson, who has a real knack for offering "forehead-slapping" solutions – "Of course! Why haven't we been doing this?"

Take but one example – what he calls the "Fundraising Menu." Here, board members are asked to generate a list of all the ways (direct and indirect) they could assist in fundraising. The list is prioritized and then used to help each trustee prepare a personalized fundraising agreement that meets his or her specific needs, interests, and limitations.

Simple, right? Yes, but few are doing it even though it's the closest thing you'll find to guaranteeing a board's commitment to raising money.

Toward the end of *Great Boards for Small Groups*, in a number of "How to Fix It" chapters, Robinson homes in on specific problems, such as poorly attended meetings, spotty follow-through on commitments, inactive board members, narrow consensus, conflicts of interest, weak agendas, and much more.

And Robinson doesn't offer up easy nostrums. Quite the opposite. Over the past 20 years, as a board member, volunteer, and consultant, he's put into practice what he preaches and stands unshakably behind his fog-burning advice.

Emerson & Church, Publishers
www.emersonandchurch.com

I've had the privilege of working with and learning from many fine trainers and consultants who teach small groups how to ask for big gifts. I could list dozens of colleagues who have generously shared their wisdom; allow me to single out just a few.

To Joan Flanagan, Kim Klein, Barbara Levy, Valerie Reuther, Mike Roque, Stephanie Roth, and my friends at the Institute for Conservation Leadership – thank you.

CONTENTS

1

The Money Taboo

I make my living as a trainer, teaching people how to raise money for charitable purposes, and I use my seminars to test ideas about fundraising.

Several years ago, at the beginning of a workshop, I took out a $20 bill and passed it around, asking, "Is this real currency?" Everyone examined the bill and agreed that yes, it was the real thing. Then, to the amazement of the group, I ripped it up. The pieces floated to the floor like confetti.

Silence – a long, profound moment of silence. They all looked at me like I was crazy.

"How did that make you feel?" I asked.

Once they started talking, they wouldn't stop. "I heard my momma's voice speaking from the grave," one woman said, "and she was telling me, 'You make him stop that!'" Several people joked, "Where's the tape?"

This was the beginning of a five-day workshop, and

to my amusement, every day that followed we had another discussion about ripping up money. It affected people in a deep, emotional way.

When they asked why I did it, I replied, "I spent one dollar per organization to get your attention. If that helps you to become more effective fundraisers and you use those contributions to change the world, that's a terrific return on my investment."

When you were growing up, what lessons did you learn about money? If you were like most kids, you probably picked up these messages:

- *Money is hard to get.* ("It doesn't grow on trees.")
- *Money is dirty.* ("Don't put that in your mouth, you don't know where it's been.")
- *Money equals power and influence.* ("When I grow up, I want to be rich.")
- *Money corrupts.* We've all heard the expression, "Money is the root of all evil," which is a misquote from the Bible. The correct verse is "The *love* of money...."
- *Money is private.* In some cultures, discussing money is even more offensive than talking about sex or death.

If you were lucky, you might have also learned you can't buy happiness or that it's good to give away money. Indeed, in some families and faith traditions, it's an *obligation* to give it away.

To be an effective fundraiser, you may need to

change your attitude about money. At the most basic level, money is neither good nor bad. There are undoubtedly corrupt ways to get it and stupid ways to spend it, but the money itself is "value-neutral."

In the old days, we used barter. I traded you a goat for a bushel of wheat. Over the centuries, we gradually replaced barter with coins and currency, though barter is still the primary means of commerce in many parts of the world. Nobody believes the goat is evil or the wheat is corrupt, so why do we ascribe these traits to pieces of paper and bits of metal?

Perhaps it will help you to think of fundraising as a kind of barter. Your donors give one thing of value – their money – in exchange for another thing of value – the good work of your organization and the benefits you provide to the community.

As a solicitor, your role is to educate your donors and learn how they want to be involved. You help them feel good about the gift. You facilitate a fair exchange.

I can't think of a more honorable job.

2

It's Simpler
Than You Think

As long as human beings have conducted commerce – we're talking thousands of years – people have been fundraising for charitable purposes (the church is one obvious example).

Indeed, our ancestors were philanthropic before money existed. They gave food to their hungry neighbors and took care of the sick.

While the idea of fundraising as a profession has only taken hold in recent years – you may in fact have a "development director" in your organization – I keep returning to something I heard Joan Flanagan say years ago.

Joan is the author of several books, including *Successful Fundraising,* and a pioneer in applying fundraising principles to the needs of grassroots organizations.

"All the knowledge about fundraising can be summed up in ten words," Joan said. "Ask 'em, thank 'em, ask 'em again, thank 'em again."

I consult with many small organizations and they find these words to be a great relief. They tend to view fundraising as complicated, mysterious, and scary. They assume they need to hire someone with appropriate credentials, as one would hire an accountant, plumber, or lawyer.

Another assumption is that professional fundraisers show up with a list of rich people who always say yes, which means volunteers won't be forced into the awkward position of asking friends, family, neighbors, and coworkers for support.

But fundraising is really pretty simple. At its heart, it is one person asking another to get involved, provide help, take a stand, join a movement, to feel good. Yes, there are strategies and techniques, but they are far less important than the one quality you need to be successful: passion for the mission.

"The best fundraisers come out of causes," says Harvey McKinnon, a consultant and author. "You can teach anyone basic skills, but you can't teach commitment and sincerity and, ultimately, that's what donors respond to."

So let me pose the crucial question: *How passionate are you?* Do you love your organization? Are you moved by its work?

If you're feeling a bit ambivalent about your group – if you're unsure about the value of the mission, the programs, or the leadership – prospective donors will sense that. All the technique in the world can't compensate for a lack of passion.

On the other hand, if you're deeply committed to your group – if you really, *really* want to see your organization succeed – you've got all the raw material you need. With a little practice, you'll be a great fundraiser.

3

The Word
You Hear Most Often

When I'm working with a group of board members or other volunteers, I often begin with an exercise. I ask people to take a blank piece of paper and draw a vertical line down the center of the page. On one side, I tell them to write a plus sign (+) and on the other a minus sign (-).

"Under the plus sign," I say, "write anything about you – your skills, your beliefs, your experience, your attitude – that's going to help you to be an effective fundraiser. I'm not asking about your organization, I'm asking about *you* – your personal qualities.

"Under the minus sign, write anything about you – your fears, your discomfort, your lack of experience, whatever – that's going to get in the way of you being successful. What are your barriers?"

After a few minutes, we discuss what people have

written. The group always compiles an impressive list of strengths. They're creative, personable, articulate, and organized. They contribute money themselves. They have sales skills. They write well. They're good listeners. Most importantly, they are passionate about their organizations.

You can probably guess the weaknesses. They have no fundraising experience, no time and no energy after a day's work. They're shy. They're disorganized. They sit on several boards, so they're fundraising (supposedly) for several groups. They don't know anyone who has money. They feel that asking for donations is impolite. They don't want to take advantage of their friends. Most of all, they're afraid of rejection – they're concerned that people will say no.

Let me make it clear from the outset: the word you hear most often in fundraising is "no." Most of the people you ask say no. That's how it works. To quote Kim Klein, author and trainer extraordinaire, "Fundraising is a volume business." You need to ask a lot of people, because most folks will turn you down.

Some 25 years ago, I began my life in fundraising as a door-to-door canvasser. Night after night, I talked with strangers about social change and asked them to join our organization. I was expected to sign up one out of every eight people.

Over the course of more than two years, I gave 10,000 pitches on 10,000 doorsteps. I did an exceptional job – I broke records for my organization – but one night, toward the end of my canvassing career, I found myself sitting on the curb, crying in the rain. The accumulated frustration of being rejected 8,800 times finally caught up with me.

You've heard this before, but if you're like me, you need to hear it again: Don't take it personally. People choose not to give for a variety of reasons – in most cases, they simply have other priorities – but it's rarely about you, the solicitor: what you said or didn't say, your clothing, your cologne, your inability to interpret body language, or your comedic timing.

You're going to be turned down. That's a fact. But here's the good news: to paraphrase Kim Klein, *you and your fellow board members and volunteers already know all the people you need to know to raise all the money you need to raise.* You have the relationships – right now – to meet your financial goals.

4

Where Money Comes From

Because money is so cloaked in secrecy and the process of asking for it makes people feel so awkward, a lot of myths about fundraising are accepted as fact. Let me try my best to debunk the most common misconceptions.

Myth: There's a shortage of money for nonprofit organizations.

Fact: Americans are extraordinarily generous.

For many years, private sector (non-government) charitable contributions in the U.S. have exceeded *$200 billion*. That's a really large number. Americans give away more money than the total economic activity of most countries.

Myth: It's impossible to raise money when the economy slows down.

Fact: Charitable giving is almost recession-proof.

Yes, private contributions dip in a bad economy, but only slightly. On the other hand, when the economy is healthy, giving expands in a big way. Taking the long view, the pool of private funding for nonprofits tends to grow over the course of several years.

Myth: The most effective way to raise money is by writing grant proposals.

Fact: The vast majority of charitable money comes from individuals.

Only 10 to 20 percent of private support is provided by foundations and corporations – the folks who read grant applications. Between 80 and 90 percent of donated dollars come from generous individuals who don't care about grant proposals. In fact, dead people, through their estates, give away more money year after year than all U.S. corporations combined.

Myth: "I don't know anyone who has money."

Fact: Roughly 70 percent of American families donate to nonprofits.

Seven out of ten people you know – your friends, neighbors, colleagues – contribute to charitable causes. Volunteer hours are not included in this calculation. We're talking cold, hard cash.

Myth: Philanthropy comes from rich people, so the best strategy is to solicit rich strangers.

Fact: People with modest incomes can, and do,

make substantial gifts.

Recent data shows that total giving per household averages about $2,000 per year. Among the two-thirds of Americans who take the standard deduction on their income taxes – primarily middle-class, working-class, and poor people – average annual donations total more than $500 per family.

●●●

We hear a lot about Packard and Turner and Gates, but a lot less about Smith, Sanchez, Lee, Nguyen, and Jones. They may not give multi-million dollar gifts, but taken as a group, they are the most predictable, reliable group of donors.

If you're looking for good prospects – generous people who care about your issues – they're right in your neighborhood. They're sitting next to you on the bus, the train, the plane ... and they're stuck in traffic, too.

If you have a job, you work with them. If you enjoy sports, you play with them (or maybe you sit on the couch and drink beer with them). If you participate in a religious congregation, you pray with them. Unless you're a hermit, you interact with donors every day – and many of them give more money than you imagine.

You know the old line about the streets being paved with gold? Surprise – this is one myth that's actually true, because philanthropists are *everywhere*.

5

Where Money Goes

Charitable giving benefits a wide range of causes and issues: social services, health care, education, the arts, the environment, youth, senior citizens, international relief and development, social justice, economic development, animal welfare, and others. Identify a need in your community – it's likely someone has created a nonprofit to address it.

When it comes to fundraising, however, one nonprofit sector outperforms all others: the faith organizations.

Year after year, churches, mosques, synagogues, temples, ashrams, and other faith communities collect more than *one-third* of all charitable dollars. They are the biggest recipients, by far, of American generosity.

Why are faith fundraisers so successful?

- *They ask.*

And ask. And ask. A typical small nonprofit operates like this: "You know, we solicited our members six months ago. We can't ask now. It's too soon. They might be offended." If churches approached fundraising in the same fashion, they would cease to exist. Many pass the plate *every week.*

- *They ask everybody.*

Faith-based organizations make little distinction between the rich and the poor. No one is screened in or out due to their *assumed* ability, or lack of ability, to give.

- *It's expected.*

There is little shame or guilt regarding "the ask." Indeed, it's accepted that everyone who attends is a donor or potential donor who would benefit by giving.

- *They provide lots of options.*

In addition to the weekly gifts solicited by some denominations, most congregations request an annual gift from their members. Then there's the building fund, overseas relief fund, social justice fund, youth development fund ... you get the idea. Everyone is expected to give, but donors have a choice in how they direct their gifts.

- *They create opportunities for donor interaction.*

Faith institutions see their constituents several times per month: at worship services, family programs, religious study, leadership meetings, and community action projects.

• *Volunteers ask for the gifts.*

Most church fundraising is built on the backs of volunteers who not only pass the plate, but lead the annual canvass of the congregation and organize fundraising events. The highest form of fundraising is peer to peer – that is, one donor soliciting another – and faith-based groups have perfected this model.

• *They do a great job building relationships.*

They know their people really, really well. When it's time to ask for the gift, these relationships pay off. While most of us can't see our donors and prospects weekly, we can and should make the effort to know them better.

●●●

Faced with the challenge of fundraising, we must learn from the masters. Those of us raising money for secular organizations would be wise to study the techniques and attitudes of the faith community.

You may not be able to equal the success of mosques, synagogues, and churches – after all, their participants demonstrate a level of commitment that few secular groups can match – but we can all learn from their methods.

6

Why $500 to $5,000?

What would you consider a "major gift" for your organization? For many grassroots groups, $100 is a strikingly large donation. For brand-name universities, the major gifts category probably begins at $5,000 or $10,000. Your group likely falls somewhere in between.

This book is designed for those of us who don't know many five, six, and seven-figure prospects. I've suggested a range of $500 to $5,000 for several reasons:

• These amounts are large enough to justify the time it takes to develop a prospect list, prepare a letter, follow with a phone call (maybe two or three) to set up the appointment, and eventually visit the prospective donor.

• These amounts are small enough to include a wide range of prospects. As a reminder, $500 per year works out to about $40 per month, which is affordable for a lot of folks if they choose to make your group a priority. (Dubious? Remember the churches.)

• These amounts are both modest enough to seem feasible to the novice, but also ambitious enough to make it worth the physical, emotional, and psychic energy required to get over all those money taboos.

• Taken in the context of a major gifts campaign, with a team of solicitors working together toward a common goal, gifts of between $500 and $5,000 can add up to a lot of money.

Having said all that, there is no particular magic attached to these numbers. You can use the strategies outlined in this book to ask your sister for $100 – though it might be simpler to just call her up – or to seek much larger donations than $5,000. You have to find your own comfort level and begin there.

If really large numbers make you nervous, start small ... but start somewhere. Not starting – in other words, not asking at all – isn't an option.

7

You, the Philanthropist

People ask you for money every day. They send you mail, call you on the phone, ring your doorbell. The girl next door (or one of her parents) sells you Girl Scout cookies. Your son wants a new pair of shoes. Even the panhandler who hangs out at the neighborhood grocery store is a fundraiser.

Philanthropy is just a fancy word for "giving away money." If you're a donor – if you belong to the 70 percent of American families that support charitable causes – congratulations! You're a philanthropist, and a lot of people want to know what makes you tick.

If you're like most folks, you give away your money for a combination of reasons:

• You care about the cause, the mission, the work of the organization.

• You see a clear need.

• You've had direct experience with the organization – perhaps you or a family member have benefited from its services.

• Giving is a tradition in your family, your faith, or your community.

• You want to "give something back."

• You want to honor or remember someone with a contribution.

• You enjoy the recognition, such as seeing your name listed in the newsletter.

• Because a friend supported your favorite cause, you feel obligated to support his.

• You itemize on your tax return and you're looking for a deduction.

• The group is throwing a fundraising party – a benefit event – and you like parties.

These are all terrific reasons to give, but the top three motivators for why you give are still missing. These are:

1) *Somebody asked.*

All fundraising begins with the simple act of one person asking another for support.

2) *You have a relationship with the asker.*

If you're asked by someone you know and trust, so much the better.

3) *You want to be a part of the work.*

People give to belong – that's why so many groups use the word "member" to describe their donors. For many contributors, the rationale goes something like this: "I would love to volunteer my time, but I am sooo busy. Here's $100 – you do it."

According to public opinion surveys, many of us find our jobs and material possessions less than satisfying, and we're looking for more meaning and connection in our lives. The chance to participate in good causes – to be part of something larger than ourselves – is deeply fulfilling.

How does charitable giving enrich your life?

8

The Day the Beggar Stopped Begging

"What do you want to learn today?" I asked the group. "How can I help you?"

A tall fellow in the back raised his hand. He had a big smile and an easy, self-assured manner. I liked him immediately. As the day went on, I discovered his career path had taken him from car salesman to Episcopal priest – quite an arc. His current passion was recruiting U.S. doctors to provide free medical care for poor children in Mexico.

"Teach me to be a better beggar," he said.

When they're new to fundraising, a lot of people feel like they're down on their knees, staring up at the donor. They feel like beggars.

As you might expect, I reject this metaphor. I see you and the donor on the same level, eye to eye. You're equals. You're negotiating a deal.

Your donors give you money, which is terrific. But look at what you're giving them: a chance to participate in the work, to ensure a critical service is provided to the community, to make the world a better place. Heck, they even get a tax break if they want it.

The definition of begging is something for nothing. The definition of fundraising is *something for something*. When you solicit a charitable gift, you're exchanging one thing of value for something else of value. The key word is *exchange*.

Supporting a good cause feels good, doesn't it? When I'm leading workshops, I often test this assumption with the participants: "How many of you have ever made a charitable gift and felt good about it?" Everyone raises their hands, of course.

This leads to another interesting question: Why are we so uncomfortable – I would even say neurotic – asking people to do something that makes them feel good when they do it? Depending on your experience and your attitude, I might have to physically force you to sit in your neighbor's kitchen and ask her for $500 ... but when she says yes, she likes it!

I have wrestled with this question for more than 20 years and can only come up with one answer. We feel uncomfortable because we believe the solicitation is about us, the askers. We focus on our discomfort. We get stuck on the money taboos.

But you know what? Fundraising is not about your

feelings – it's about the donor. As a solicitor, your job is to reach out with integrity – to make a clear case for your organization, to listen carefully, to engage the prospect on as many levels as you can. Your job is to serve the donor.

In the end, how *you* feel is much less important than how your contributors feel. If you approach the process with honesty and humility, you're going to feel fine. With practice, you might even learn to enjoy it.

9

"I Can't Ask My Friends!"

"How many of you," I say, "would be uncomfortable asking friends and family to donate to your favorite group?"

Most of the people in the room – dozens and dozens of them – raise their hands.

"Why?"

"I don't want to take advantage of my friends," says one.

"I don't want to be seen as mercenary," responds another. "Friendship and money don't mix."

"They're going to turn around and ask me to support *their* groups," says a third, and everyone laughs appreciatively. "I can't afford to say yes to everyone."

"How many of you have done it anyway?" I ask.

Nearly every hand goes up.

"So has anyone ever lost or damaged a friendship

because of a charitable request?"

The room goes quiet. We all look at each other, sitting on our hands.

I've asked this question of thousands of people. Perhaps one out of 50 will talk about a friendship gone sour due to miscommunication or inappropriate expectations. The other 49 of us sit silently, wondering why our fears are so disconnected from reality.

Most of us have been raised to solve our own problems and not trouble anyone else. Independence, we've been told, is the great American virtue. Asking for help somehow implies we're not clever enough or strong enough – it's a sign of weakness. We fear it will obligate us to do something in return that we don't really want to do.

Let's be honest – when we're raising money, we *are* asking for help. If we individually had enough money or energy or power to solve community problems alone, we'd probably just do it ourselves.

Unfortunately, big challenges such as poverty, disease, and injustice require big solutions. None of us can solve them individually. We need each other.

Let me suggest a way of asking that might ease your mind. "Maxine," you say, "I'm involved with a great cause. We're doing terrific work to improve our community and we need your help. If you could support us with a $500 donation, it would mean a great deal to me. If you choose not to participate, that's OK – we'll still be friends no matter what. But I sure hope you can help."

In other words, when you ask, you give the person explicit permission to say no. There's no pressure involved.

Given your passion and the power of your cause, some will say yes. I promise you that they will be grateful for the opportunity to participate.

10

"But I Don't Know Anyone Who Has Money!"

Almost a decade ago, after several positions with a variety of grassroots groups, I left a steady job to start a consulting practice.

Financially speaking, I leapt into the void. My wife was working at the time, finishing up a long career as a Montessori preschool teacher – another highly paid profession. The two of us, working full-time, had a combined income of about $35,000, which I guess landed us somewhere in the middle class.

We gave away money: $25 to one group, $50 to another, sometimes as much as $100. At the end of the year I added up our donations and discovered we had contributed a total of $2,500. That startled me. I added the numbers twice, because I didn't believe it.

Apparently we were "major donors."

Let me tell you about our lives. We lived with our daughter in a tiny rented house; a sweet and comfy home, but less than one thousand square feet. Many of my trousers were (and are) frayed, because I hate to go shopping. I drove a 1981 Toyota with 200,000 miles and no air conditioning – in Tucson, Arizona. If you saw me in that car, the last thing you would have said is, "There goes a major donor!"

I'm happy to report that business is good. I now earn about twice what my wife and I used to earn together, which has made it possible for her to stop working. We have a policy of tithing, or giving away 10 percent of our earnings. In a recent year, this totaled about $7,500 in charitable donations distributed among nearly one hundred groups.

Until a few years ago, when we abandoned the desert for the woods of Vermont, I continued to drive my hard-working (and very warm) Toyota because, among other reasons, I wanted to prove a point. There's only one way to figure out how much money individuals can give you – and it's *not* what they drive, *not* where they live, *not* what they wear. You don't have access to your neighbor's bank statement, right? The only way to find out how much someone can give you is to *ask*.

In my ongoing campaign to demystify fundraising, I tell a lot of groups about my income, car, house, giving, and so on, and it generates some interesting responses.

One man stood up and talked about his grandfather, a farmer in North Dakota. "He lives pretty simply," he said, "but I know he supports his favorite organizations. If my grandfather knew that people were sitting across town saying, 'We can't ask Pete for money. He's too poor. Look at his tractor,' it would make him crazy. He would say, 'Have you studied my checkbook? Have you looked at my bank account? *How dare you make that decision for me.*'"

So let's keep this simple. Fundraising boils down to two jobs:

- The **asker** – that's you – asks for the gift.

- The **decider** says, "Yes, I choose to give," or "No, I'm sorry, I choose not to give."

Do not confuse these two jobs. Don't make decisions for other people based on your extremely limited knowledge of their finances. Don't screen them in or out based on rumor, hearsay, or the condition of their automobiles.

You may have seen a story in the *New York Times* that profiled the work of two philanthropists: Ted Turner (you know who he is) and Oseola McCarty, an African-American woman from Mississippi. She made her living as a domestic worker, taking in laundry.

When she reached her eighties, she donated her life savings – $150,000! – to create a scholarship fund for black students at the local university. "I can't do everything," she said, "but I can do something to help somebody. And what I can do, I will do. I wish I could do more."

When you hear "major donor" and "philanthropist," you probably don't think of people like Oseola McCarty, and that's too bad. For every story like hers featured in the news media, hundreds of thousands remain untold.

Remember, 70 percent of American families donate to nonprofits. You're surrounded by philanthropists. Knowing people who *have money* is irrelevant; the question is, do you know people who *give money*?

Of course you do. And you won't know how much they can give until you ask.

11

Prospecting: Looking Beyond the Locals

We often use the word *prospect* to describe potential donors. Generally speaking, prospects meet the following criteria, which are arranged in order of importance:

• **Contact:** Do they have *relationships* with you, other board members, staff, key volunteers, or other donors to your group? A direct personal relationship is best, but an indirect relationship – for example, a friend in common who opens the door – is often sufficient.

• **Belief:** Do they *care* about your cause, issue, programs, or constituency?

• **Ability:** Do they have *money* or other resources to give? It's wise to assume the answer is yes, since you won't really know until you ask.

People who meet these three criteria are *prospects*

and should be asked for support.

According to demographers, the average American adult knows roughly 200 people. It's unlikely that every one is a legitimate prospect – indeed, many may be children or folks you haven't seen in 20 years – but you know a lot more potential donors than you realize. When your colleagues start adding the names of people they know, the list gets pretty large.

The typical board of directors, working moderately hard, should be able come up with at least 500 bona fide prospects. They won't all be $1,000 leads – many will turn out to be $50 donors – but the relationships are there, if you and your fellow board members will put your heads together.

When looking for prospects, it's appropriate to begin with your neighbors, since you probably have the strongest relationships with people who live in your community. These folks are most affected by the problem you're trying to solve. They're the ones most likely to use your services.

However, savvy fundraisers understand that relationships are more important than geography. Don't limit yourself to the locals. In compiling your prospect list, consider the following folks.

• *Former locals.* About twenty percent of Americans move each year, but many retain ties to their former homes. Children grow up and move away, but still feel connected to the places they were raised. Even if they see no direct benefit from your work, these people appreciate what you do from a distance.

• *Friends and family elsewhere.* Stay in touch with family and friends who live somewhere else. They might surprise you.

• *Part-time locals.* Many rural areas include second home owners. Some of these folks spend long periods in their second home: Florida all winter, Maine all summer, and so on. Others visit their vacation home nearly every weekend and holiday. Many second home owners intend to move or retire there and identify strongly with the landscape, people, and values of their adopted community. Given their financial circumstances – it's not cheap maintaining two residences – these people are also candidates for major gifts.

Keep flipping through your mental Rolodex. (Going through your real Rolodex, personal database, or little black book is a good idea too.) Who do you know who might be willing to help?

12

Thy Neighbor's Donor

If the word you hear most often in fundraising is "no," then my vote for the most annoying word is "competition." With more than one million nonprofits in the U.S., it's undeniably true that donors have a lot of options. They also have to sort through a maddening degree of duplication, since thousands upon thousands of organizations have overlapping missions.

Unfortunately, "competition" implies winners and losers fighting for finite resources. As I hope you've seen by now, philanthropic scarcity is a myth – there's plenty of money to take care of us all, especially if you're willing to invest some time and energy in the $500 to $5,000 neighborhood.

Most people who give away money spread it around. According to some studies, the typical donor family supports five to eight organizations per year, and millions of contributors support ten or more charities annually. They often cluster their giving by category: some focus on the arts, others on health, still others on education or the environment.

So how do you find the names of likely supporters outside of your immediate circle or network?

Fortunately, most nonprofits are nice enough to acknowledge their donors in their newsletters, annual reports, event programs, and other publications. They often sort their donors by gift levels – Benefactor, Angel, Archangel, Supreme Deity – which gives you a pretty clear idea about how much each person contributes.

To expand your own prospect pool, consider the following:

• Contact all nonprofits operating in your area whose mission or constituency overlaps yours in any way, including local, regional, and national organizations. Ask for their most recent annual report and request to be put on their mailing list for newsletters. If they only distribute newsletters to paid members, consider a donation to join the group.

• Photocopy donor lists from these publications and share them with your board, staff, key volunteers, and significant contributors. Ask them to mark off any names they know, especially if they have postal addresses, phone numbers, and/or e-mail addresses.

• Compare these lists to your own. If you see any of your supporters, note how much they give to other groups. With luck, you'll discover that some of your

$50 members are giving $500 or more to other organizations. These folks should be prioritized for major gifts visits.

If you diligently collect lists and "screen" names, your fundraising effort will benefit in at least two ways: you'll have lots of people to solicit, and you'll begin to build your fundraising team by engaging board, staff, and volunteers in the process.

13

The Most Effective Way to Ask

If you've read this far, you'll understand that the most effective way to raise money is face to face. This strategy has several advantages:

• You can talk with prospects to learn how their interests dovetail with the work of your organization.

• By communicating your passion for the mission, you make the case in a personal way.

• You can respond directly to questions or concerns.

• You can bring visual aids – maps, charts, photos, site plans, or blueprints.

• It demonstrates your commitment to the cause. Not only are you giving your time and money, you're showing courage by meeting with donors to solicit their support.

When making visits to your prospects, in most cases

you'll have better luck going out in teams of two. Novices are sometimes afraid the donor will feel "ganged up on" when two solicitors come to call, but the advantages far outweigh any potential problems.

• In the traditional model, one solicitor – often a board member – "opens the door," while the other solicitor – typically a staff member – provides more detailed knowledge of the program.

• At any given moment, one of you can be the "designated listener" and fully concentrate on what the prospect is saying, rather than thinking three steps ahead in the conversation.

• It helps to ensure continuity with the donor. If one solicitor moves on to a new job or a new city, someone within your group (the other solicitor) still knows the donor on a face-to-face basis.

• Prospects are sometimes flattered by the attention: "They sent a delegation to see me, so I must be important."

• Finally, two solicitors strengthen each other's resolve and provide moral support.

Regardless of whether you make these visits alone or bring a colleague along, do everything you can to meet with your donors and prospective donors in person.

14

If You Don't Have a Goal, You Won't Reach It

When raising money from individuals, we're concerned about two sets of numbers: how many *donors* participate and how many *dollars* they contribute. In a typical annual campaign,

• The top 10 percent of your donors contribute 60 percent of the financial goal;

• The next 20 percent of donors contribute 20 percent of the goal;

• The remaining 70 percent of donors provide the balance: 20 percent of the goal.

In other words, most organizations rely on a handful of major donors to generate the majority of their unrestricted income. Using this principle, you can set a campaign goal and then calculate how many donations at each level you'll need to meet that goal.

With the title of this book as a guide, it would be possible to create a $50,000 gift chart focusing on major gifts of $500 to $5,000.

GIFT RANGE	#GIFTS	#PROSPECTS	TOTAL $/RANGE
$5,000	3	15 (5:1)	$15,000
$2,500	5	25 (5:1)	$12,500
$1,000	12	48 (4:1)	$12,000
$ 500	21	63 (3:1)	$10,500

This is a flexible model, so adapt it to your own circumstances. Note the ratios: 5:1, 4:1 and 3:1. These are estimates, but the implication is clear: for every $5,000 donor, you will need to identify about five $5,000 prospects.

After you have compiled a list of prospects, a team of board, staff, and other solicitors come together to review the list, match prospects to amounts, and assign them to solicitors. This is often called "rating" the prospects. For example, the expanded internal version of the first line of the chart would look like this:

GIFT RANGE	#GIFTS	#PROSPECTS	TOTAL $/RANGE	PROSPECTS	SOLICITORS
$5,000	3	15 (5:1)	$15,000	1_____	_____
				2_____	_____
				3_____	_____

(continue list to include 15 slots)

Prospect rating is an exercise in organized gossip. "Ed, you put Sandy Yang on your list. How much do you think we should ask her for? Does anyone else know Sandy – maybe you have an opinion? Okay, let's put her down for $____. Ed, are you willing to be the solicitor? Great – who would like to help Ed with that one?"

Bring lots of pizza and beverages, because the process takes awhile. It's also a good way to test the feasibility of your goal. From the sample chart above, it should be evident that you'll need lots of prospects – roughly 150 in this case – so you'll want lots of helpers combing through donor lists, thinking about their own contacts, and compiling names.

As mentioned before, fundraising is a volume business. If you can't fill all the slots – in other words, if you're lacking enough prospects, solicitors, or both – you may have to lower your sights or delay your campaign.

15

Before You Ask Others, Give Money Yourself

There's karma in fundraising, and I can pretty much guarantee that if you're not giving, you're not getting.

I don't believe in setting board quotas – in other words, "Every board member has to give at least $1,000" – but I strongly believe that all board members must give to the best of their abilities. Here's appropriate language: "Because you're a leader in this organization, we expect to be one of the top three charities you support this year."

There's no way to enforce this – you're not going to subpoena everyone's checkbooks – but it sets the right tone. It also means that if $100 is a stretch for you, your organization should graciously accept your check for $100 or perhaps your commitment of $8 per month.

Maybe you're one of those board members who say,

"I give my time, which is more valuable, so why should I give money, too?" You're right about the time commitment: it *is* more valuable than money. But in your role as board member you need to give both time and money. Here's why.

• Fundraising is part of your job, and you'll be more effective if you do what you're asking others to do.

• Despite what you've heard, time and money are *not* convertible – neither the phone company nor the landlord are willing to accept your time in lieu of cash.

• Sooner or later, you'll be asked this question by an individual prospect, foundation officer, or corporate funder: "How many of your board members give to the organization?" And if you can't say, "One hundred percent – every single one of us!" the prospect will reply, "Well, if you can't get your own folks to give, why should I?"

To put it bluntly, board members who refuse to financially support their own organizations can end up costing their groups a lot more money than they can potentially give themselves. Before you ask others, please be as generous as you can be.

16

Honesty, Follow-through, and Reasonable Expectations

The process of soliciting a big gift generally includes three stages:

1) A *letter* requesting a meeting.

2) A *phone call* following the letter to set up an appointment.

3) A *visit* to solicit the gift.

The remainder of this book will walk you through each stage in more detail. But before we travel that road together, I must emphasize three key points.

• *Honesty and transparency generate the best results.* At each stage – letter, phone call, and visit – you must be completely clear about your purpose, which is to raise money for your organization. If you ambush people – if you go to see them on other pretenses and then spring the fundraising question like a loaded trap – you will annoy them and consequently not raise much money.

"Transparency" means naming numbers right from the start: "Alice, I am writing because we're launching our first major gifts campaign and we're looking for gifts of $500 to $5,000. I'm not sure how much to ask you for, so let's sit down together and talk about it."

• *Don't start what you can't finish.* Once you begin, you must follow through. The worst thing you can do is to mail a letter to a prospect that says, "I will call you," and then studiously avoid the telephone.

If you plan to lose your nerve, do so before you begin. The credibility of your organization (not to mention your personal credibility) depends on you and your teammates honoring your commitments.

• *Begin with reasonable expectations.* The beauty of a straightforward approach is that it screens out those who are less likely to give. True, you will lose some candidates at each stage, but the ones who remain will be strong prospects.

If you start with a letter that focuses on fundraising, and follow up with a phone call that also explicitly mentions fundraising, any prospects who agree to meet will seriously consider your request before you even walk in the door. Furthermore, if you mention numbers in advance, they won't be shocked by the amounts when you sit down together.

As for what you might expect, if you send 10 letters to legitimate prospects, you will eventually reach six or seven by phone, and three to five will agree to meet.

As they say in the commercials, your results may vary. With persistence and a little luck, they may be significantly better.

17

Act I:
The Letter

Let's imagine you're writing to a current donor to set up an appointment.

Dear Martina:

It's that time of year again – we're doing our annual fundraising campaign in support of (brief description of your mission). Last year, you made a very generous donation of $500, which is a big gift for us, and we really appreciate your support. Contributions from people like you helped us to accomplish the following:

- (Big, impressive accomplishment)
- (Not so big, but still impressive)
- (Something interesting the donor is unlikely to know about)

This year, we face a number of challenges:

- (Big, scary challenge – maybe increased demand for your services?)

- (Not so big, but still impressive)
- (Perhaps something about building your organization, rather than providing services or doing advocacy work)

To meet these challenges, we're asking our most generous supporters to consider doubling their gifts, which in your case would be a contribution of $1,000. I appreciate that this is a big commitment, so before you decide, I'd love the chance to meet with you, give you an update, learn more about your interest in our work, and ask for your support.

I'll be calling you next week to set up an appointment.

Again, thank you for your generous and loyal support. I look forward to speaking with you, and meeting with you, very soon.

Warm regards,

If you're uncomfortable specifying a number, consider language like this:

We're asking for gifts of between $500 and $5,000 toward a campaign goal of $50,000. To be honest, I'm not sure how much to ask you for, so let's sit down together, discuss it, and you can tell me what amount would be appropriate.

Some of my nonprofit colleagues use words like "financial support" without mentioning any numbers in the letter. This approach is certainly acceptable. However, in my experience fundraising works best when everyone starts the discussion with similar expectations.

If you're writing to a prospect, rather than a donor, the relevant paragraphs might be:

> As you might know, I'm on the board of the local food bank, which works to (brief description of your mission). Our organization has a long history of success, including (insert bulleted items here).
>
> One of my tasks as a board member is to identify new supporters for our work. We've set a goal of $____ and we're seeking donations of between $____ and $____ to help meet that goal. I'd like to arrange an appointment so we can discuss the work and see if you'd like to contribute.

While I have provided sample language, please avoid the easy shortcut of simply using this letter. You'll be more effective if you adapt the language and tone as you see fit. Just keep the following points in mind:

- *It's brief* – no more than one page.
- *It says "thank you."* It acknowledges past support or, in the case of new prospects, it thanks them for considering a gift.
- *It's explicitly about fundraising.* It doesn't hint or use code words – your intentions are clear from the

start.

• *It includes numbers.* It mentions the amount you seek or suggests a range of gifts. (As mentioned above, this point is optional but recommended.)

• *The purpose of this letter isn't to get money, but rather to get a meeting.*

It's not necessary to craft a piece of great literature – after all, this is a one-page "I want to meet with you" letter – so don't strive for perfection. It might make sense for one person, perhaps a staff member, to prepare a standard letter that board members and other solicitors then customize. Get it done and mail it out.

18

Act II:
The Phone Call

For many solicitors, the phone call is the hardest stage in the process. In our society, we often consider anything that combines telephones with money as telemarketing, which seems universally despised. Fair enough...but allow me to make a not-so-subtle point.

The definition of telemarketing is one stranger calling another. You won't be doing that. You'll be calling friends, family members, colleagues, co-workers, and neighbors. Perhaps you'll be lucky enough to contact your organization's donors, members, and volunteers – people who have already expressed their commitment by contributing time, money, or both. *These are not cold calls. This is not telemarketing.*

The telephone is a fabulous tool for raising money (as long you don't call complete strangers), but it does have limitations:

• You can't see people, so it's impossible to respond to their body language. Are they leaning forward with anticipation? Are they rolling their eyes in frustration?

• Because talking by phone is less personal than meeting face-to-face, it's much easier for the prospect to turn down your request.

• Many individuals screen their calls or simply don't pick up the phone.

To succeed, you'll need to be persistent and flexible. Call at different times of day and different days of the week. I'd suggest that you call four or five times and leave three voice messages before giving up on a prospect. The message goes something like this:

> "Hi Mike, this is Rodrigo. I'm following up on the letter I sent last week about our fundraising campaign. I'm hoping to schedule a time for us to meet. Please give me a call at 555-5555. If I don't hear back from you in the next few days, I'll try again. Thanks."

If four or five calls seem like too many, then call three times before you give up. Find your own comfort level. However, calling once, leaving a message, and then writing off the prospect isn't good fundraising – it's fear or laziness.

You can overcome that. You're doing an important job and as long as you're honest, humble, and responsive, no one will think poorly of you. Indeed, many will admire you.

If you're not getting through on the phone, e-mail provides another option. Some fundraisers find that e-mail offers the best option for scheduling appointments, though it has the same drawbacks as the phone: it's a bit impersonal and easy to ignore. Having said that, effective solicitors use every tool in the toolbox before giving up on a prospect.

19

Do I Hear Any Objections?

Sooner or later you will have this experience. After a few words of explanation – "Hi Leroy, this is Andy Robinson. I'm following up on the letter I sent about our fall fundraising campaign" – the person on the other end of the phone will say, "Sure, Andy, I'd love to get together. When's a good time for you?" Until that day, however, you must learn to respond to the most common objections.

I don't mean to imply that the following responses constitute one conversation and you have to handle eight or nine put-offs in a row. However, the general rule is that you should respond to at least three before giving up.

Objection: "I don't have time to talk right now."
Response: "When would be a good time to call?"

Objection: "You sent me a letter? What letter?"

(Or alternatively, "There's a pile of mail on the kitchen table – bills and such – and I've been avoiding it.")

Response: "Well, let me tell you about the letter."

Objection: "I don't really have the time to meet. Can't we just do this over the phone?"

Response: "That's up to you. The meeting takes about 20 minutes, and I'll make it as convenient as possible – I can come to your home or office, whatever works for you. This just works better if we meet face to face."

Objection: "I can't afford the amount you're asking for."

Response: "The amount is completely up to you. Let's sit down together, discuss it, and then you'll decide."

Objection: "You know, I generally make charitable decisions with my spouse/partner/financial advisor/eight year old child/psychic friend."

Response: "Is it appropriate for the three of us to sit down together? If so, when would be a good time? If not, how can I help you to have that discussion – maybe the two of us could meet first?"

Objection: "You know, I support so many other groups and I'm tapped out for the year."

Response: "I know the feeling. Tell you what – let's

take the money off the table. I'd still like to meet to thank you for your generous support last year. When you're budgeting for next year, perhaps you could remember us then. So let's assume you won't be giving now – I hear that. But I'd still like to meet. When would be a good time?"

Objection: "I gave because of your work on _____, but I don't like the position you've taken on _____."

Response: "You know, I'd like to hear more about your concerns. Frankly, I don't like everything the organization does either, but overall I believe the mission and the work are important. Let's get together and talk about it, and then you'll decide. If you choose not to give, I certainly respect that. When would be a good time to meet?"

Objection: "We're down to one income and we don't have the money."

Response: "I'm sorry to hear that. Is there some other way you'd like to be involved in our work?"

Objection: "This just isn't a priority right now."

Response: "Well, your past support has meant a lot to us. Shall we keep you on the mailing list? Is it appropriate to contact you again in the future?"

●●●

You're probably thinking, "What's wrong with this guy? Can't he take 'no' for an answer?"

I would respond as follows. When people say no – "We don't have the money" or "This is not a priority right now" – I hear them say no and honor that.

But when they say, "That's more than I can afford," or "I have to talk with my spouse first," that doesn't mean they don't want to give – it means they want to choose the amount or would prefer to consult with someone else before making a decision.

Therefore, the *Three Rules of Telephone Appointment-Making:*

1) *Whatever the objection, take it literally.* Rather than making assumptions about what other people mean and trying to read between the lines, take them at their word.

2) *Assume success.* Don't ask, "Do you want to meet?" Say, "*When* do you want to meet?" This is a subtle distinction, but it makes a big difference.

3) *Keep bringing it back to your agenda.* "When would be a good time to meet?"

Strive for a balance between assertiveness and humility, between boldness and fear. If you give in to fear – if you backpedal at the first objection – you do a disservice to yourself, your group, and your donors. Be bold and watch what happens.

20

Where Do We Meet?

Wondering about best place to meet your prospect or donor? Here are four options, in order of preference.

1) At his or her home. This is the first priority for several reasons.

• People are most comfortable in their own environment, and comfort encourages generosity.

• You can learn a lot about people from their material circumstances – the nature of their homes or apartments, the items hanging on the wall, their family members and pets, all of which can be conversation starters.

• It's easier to linger and have a more substantive discussion in one's home.

2) At his or her workplace. This has some of the same advantages as home, but also several disadvantages – more competition for the person's focus and potentially more interruptions ("You have an important call on line two.")

3) At your organization. On the one hand, donors or would-be donors have to make a greater effort to meet you on your own turf and may feel less at ease once they arrive.

On the other hand, you'll have great "show and tell" opportunities. Your venue could be a nature preserve, theater, child care center, rehabilitation facility, classroom ... even a picket line or public hearing. When people can see and feel your work firsthand, it lifts them up and makes them want to participate.

4) At a neutral location, typically a restaurant. Novice solicitors assume that fundraising calls typically take place over public meals. This is the least favorable option because:

• Food – especially disappointing food – can get in the way of the discussion.

• You can't control the environment. Consider, for example, the unhappy child at the next table or the uproarious drunken party in the corner booth.

• Then there's the awkward business of who buys the meal. In fact, it's guaranteed that just when you're winding up to make your pitch, the waiter arrives with the check.

Neutral locations are great for getting to know prospects or reporting to donors on how you spent their money. As venues for soliciting gifts, however, use them as a last resort.

21

Act III:
The Visit

Believe it or not, you'll actually get to meet with some of your donors and prospects. What follows is a brief overview of the meeting. In subsequent chapters, many of these components are covered in more detail.

1) Build rapport. Chat a little. Start with topics that have no bearing on your organization or fundraising campaign. "How's your job? What are your kids doing these days? I notice you've got your garden in; what are you growing this year?" Don't spend a lot of time on idle chatter – the meeting might get away from you – but it's good manners to ease into the topic at hand.

2) State your goals for the meeting. This step is optional but recommended. You might say, "Margarita, I've come today with three things on my mind. One, I'm here to tell you about our work. Two, I want to

learn more about you and your interests. Three, it's my responsibility to ask for your financial support. To tell you the truth, I'd like to know why you're interested in our organization, so let's start there." This provides a clean segue into the next item.

3) Uncover the person's needs and interests. Find out why he or she cares about your work. For a donor, the questions might be, "You gave us $500 last year, which is a big gift for us. Why did you do it? Why do you care about this issue?" When talking with a prospect who is considering a first gift to your group, perhaps you can ask, "What's your experience with our work? Why does it interest you?" Initiate a dialogue by asking questions. Get the prospect talking.

4) Present your organization: your goals, programs, and financial needs. Tell stories. Where relevant, cite statistics. Keep it brief; don't overwhelm the person with a blow-by-blow description of your 14-point strategic plan. If you have visuals that tell your story – maps, graphs, photos, charts, or site plans – this is an opportunity to use them. Always encourage questions.

5) Ask for the gift. Be clear, explicit, and straightforward. "Sally, as I mentioned in the letter, we were hoping you'd consider a gift of $1,000 to support our work. It would mean a lot to us. What do you say?" As an alternative, "As I mentioned in the letter, we're

looking for gifts of between $500 and $5,000. I appreciate that this is a wide range, and to be honest, we don't know the appropriate amount to ask of you. How much would you like to give?"

Once you've asked for the gift, wait – keep your mouth closed. Don't make excuses or start to backpedal before the donor has a chance to respond. Just sit quietly and wait.

6) Deal with any objections. Some of the objections you answered by phone are likely to come up again now. Think in advance about these objections and how you might respond. Practice your answers and bring notes to the meeting. For example, if the person says, "You're asking for more than I can afford," you can reply, "How much would you like to give?" In response to, "I'm unable to give right now," you could say, "Do you want to make a pledge now and pay later? If that works for you, it works for us." Most of these responses are nothing more than common sense, so:

• Take a breath,

• Ask yourself, "What's the logical response to this concern?"

• Respond accordingly.

7) Close the meeting. Restate any agreements you've made so both parties leave the room with the same expectations. Once again, be clear, explicit, and straightforward.

22

Two Ears, One Mouth

Major gifts fundraising is more about listening than talking. Solicitors who talk too much tend to fail.

Novices are the worst offenders. They're filled with nervous energy. They're uncomfortable with silence and work doubly hard to carry the conversation. They mistakenly believe that, once armed with the perfect "case," they can talk somebody into giving – so they obsess about getting the language right. They assume that the donor's decision is based on the pitch.

You cannot talk someone into giving you money. In fact, you can talk them out of giving by talking too much.

On the other hand, you can *listen someone into giving* by asking good questions, being fully present in the conversation, and listening carefully to what he or she has to say. Fundraising guru Jerry Panas calls this "listening the gift," and it's the most important skill in face to face fundraising.

As you've learned, fundraising isn't about money – it's about relationships. Think about your own relationships. How do you feel when friends or family members talk too much and monopolize the conversation? Or when they get excited about their interests and passions and problems, but never ask about yours? Would you rather listen to a monologue or join a dialogue?

Thanks to millions of years of evolution and the grace of God, you've been given two ears and one mouth. That's no accident. When you're meeting with donors or prospects, try to listen twice as much as you talk.

Engage the person by preparing questions in advance and bringing them to the meeting.

• Why are you interested in our work?

• What's your experience with our issue – has someone you know been affected?

• (For current donors) Last year, you gave $____. Why did you do it? What is it about our work that moves you?

• What are your favorite organizations? Why?

• When you make a donation, how do you like to be acknowledged?

I'm not suggesting you conduct an interrogation, so don't come on too strong. Your job is to stimulate a dialogue, and the best way to do that is to ask questions.

It won't surprise you to know that people like to talk about themselves, so make it easy. *The more they talk, the better your chance of getting the gift* – not because you manipulate them, but because you're genuinely interested in their point of view. If you know what motivates them, you'll be a more responsive partner.

23

Show and Tell

One of the great advantages of asking face-to-face is that you can show your stuff – literally. You don't need glossy, full-color materials to impress donors, but if you can find ways to present your work visually, it will add another dimension to the discussion.

Are you building a new facility? Bring along your architectural drawings and site plans. Launching a public education campaign? Show the design for your new billboard. Does your mission involve children, housing, pets, art, food, job training, wildlife, theater, senior citizens – in other words, do you have any good photos you can share?

Maps are especially useful for organizations whose work can be represented geographically. For example, maps can show how air pollution from the factory affects the local neighborhood, or the ways that your new location will help you better serve your clients.

I'm not suggesting that fancy visuals are required.

Do not delay your fundraising campaign for months while you argue about brochures, photographs, or newsletter design.

In the end, these materials may be more important to the solicitor than the prospect. They provide an aura of credibility. They serve as tools to keep the conversation on track and moving toward "the ask." A good packet can give the psychological boost needed to get over the fear of asking.

Finally, visual materials help to counter a common objection. If a prospect says, "We don't need to meet. Why don't we just discuss this over the phone?" you can respond, "You know, I've got some great materials to show you, and I just can't do that on the phone. So let's get together – I promise it won't take long. When would be a good time?"

24

Name that Number

For many of us, the hardest part of asking for the gift is naming the number. We hint, we stammer, we offer subtle suggestions like, "Please be as generous as you can," and then pray we'll be overwhelmed with a huge gift.

Sometimes people will bail us out with a direct question: "How much did you have in mind?" (If this happens, you better have a number handy.) In most cases, however, it falls to the asker – that means you – to state the amount you want them to give.

As suggested earlier, a few simple strategies can help you determine the amount.

• Study the donor's past giving to your organization, including how the person was asked. Assume that, when solicited face to face, contributors can give five to ten times what they typically donate through the mail.

• Examine his or her contributions to other

nonprofits as listed in their annual reports, newsletters, event programs, and other publications.

• Hold a screening and rating session, during which you discuss the prospect or donor and arrive at what seems to be an appropriate amount.

When phrasing the request, there are no magic words, but here are a few options:

> "Louisa, we've set a goal of $50,000 for our major gifts campaign. To start the campaign, we're looking for three people to give lead gifts of $5,000. We're asking you to be one of those people."

Or try this:

> "Antonio and I pledged $500, which is a lot of money for us. We're asking five of our friends, including you, to do the same. Will you participate? It would sure mean a lot to us."

Or maybe:

> "As I said in the letter, we're asking you to consider a gift of $2,000 this year. I sure hope you can help."

If you're having a hard time finding the right number, try this strategy. Hand your gift pyramid (see Appendix A) to the person and say,

> "As I mentioned in the letter, we're seeking

donations of between $500 and $5,000. When all the boxes are filled in, we'll reach our goal. To be honest, we don't know how much to ask you for, so perhaps you can give us some guidance. Please take a look at the chart and choose a number that feels right to you."

Using the gift chart offers several advantages:

• You don't have to actually name the number. You can simply pick a box on the pyramid, point to it, and ask, "How about this one?"

• You look organized and professional. Your plan is clear: when all the slots are claimed, it adds up to your goal.

• If the donor chooses to "negotiate down," you control the terms of the negotiation by setting the giving levels.

• Finally, the pyramid provides an opportunity for donor recognition. After the prospect chooses an amount, you can say, "May we put your name on the chart to let other people know you have pledged $____?" Some contributors will be pleased to have you include their name; others will prefer to be anonymous.

Faced with a range of choices, some donors will disappoint you by choosing the smallest number available (so don't include a $50 option). On the other hand, some will surprise and delight you by making larger gifts than you would have thought possible.

25

The Gift of Silence

If you think naming the amount is difficult, try asking for the contribution and then remaining silent. It's hard to do, but if you're going to succeed, it's essential.

Novice solicitors tend to stammer out the number and then immediately backpedal before the prospect has a chance to consider the request. If you're not careful, your mouth will open against your will and all sorts of inappropriate comments will come out.

• "I know that's a lot of money. You really don't have to give that much."

• "I know this is a bad time for you, because it's certainly a bad time for me."

• "You don't have to decide right now."

• "Of course, if you're as broke as I am, there's no way you could even consider a gift of that size."

• "I'd like to crawl under a rock and die from embarrassment. Care to join me?"

Let's look past your discomfort for a moment and enter the mind of the prospect. Because of your transparent approach, this person knows – long before the meeting – the purpose of your visit and roughly how much money you're seeking. He or she will be neither shocked nor upset when you ask for the gift. Indeed, the individual may be wishing that you'd gotten around to the point ten minutes earlier.

So you ask. And you wait. And while you wait, your prospective donor is silently juggling the following questions.

• Is this a priority for me? Is my interest in this group or this issue worth this much?

• Do I have the money now or will I need to budget this gift over time?

• If I choose to make the gift now, do I have to transfer funds between accounts?

• How will this donation affect my other financial obligations, including the other charities I support?

• Do I know of any unusual expenses (car repair, tuition payment, home improvement) that are coming up soon?

• Who else do I need to talk with to help me figure this out?

It's a lot to think about, and it takes a while to work through all these questions. Rather than fill the space with your anxious chatter, sit quietly and give the prospect the gift of silence to figure it out. If you feel the need to occupy yourself, sip your drink. You don't have to stare the person down; it's fine to break eye contact and look away. If necessary, dig your fingernails into your kneecaps to distract yourself.

The main point is this: ask for the gift and wait with your mouth shut. If you take nothing else from this book, please remember to ask and then be quiet.

26

There are Only Three Answers to the Question, "Will You Help Us?"

When you ask for the gift, the donor can only respond three ways.

1) Yes. If you get a "yes" – and sooner or later you will – it's acceptable to act surprised. It's even better to act delighted. Be enthusiastic – show your gratitude.

After saying thank you, figure out how the contribution will be made. Follow-up questions could include:

- "How would you like to pay?"
- "Would you like to write us a check today? If you prefer, we also accept credit cards."
- "Shall I send you an invoice?"

• "Would you like to pay in installments? For example, we could set up quarterly payments."

Once the logistics have been worked out, be sure to restate any agreements before you leave the meeting.

2) No. Sometimes a "no" is unequivocal – "I'm sorry, this just isn't a priority now" – in which case it's appropriate to thank them for their interest and explore whether they'd like to stay in touch with the organization. At other times, you can use the "no" to reframe your request.

"I'm sorry, but you're asking for more than we can afford."

Response: "How much would you like to give?"

Or:

"Financially speaking, this is not the best moment."

Response: "I know how that feels. Would you like to pledge now and pay later? If that's something you want to do, we can arrange it."

Listen carefully to the prospect's words. Remember, whatever he or she says, take it *literally.* If you do that, you'll sense when to continue or back off.

3) Maybe, I'm not sure, let me think about it. Some people will decide not to decide. Rather than applying pressure, explore what they need to make a good choice. For example, you could ask, "Do you want more information? Is there anything else I can tell you about our organization?"

When you come to a "maybe," your goal is to negotiate a next step that involves the prospect and moves him or her closer to a decision. You might say,

• "I'd love to give you a tour of our school/forest preserve/medical center/museum/food bank. Come see the work for yourself. If you want to stop in for lunch one day, I'll bring the sandwiches. Let's schedule it now, what do you say?"

• "Why don't I leave you with these materials and you can think about it. I'll check in later and you can tell me what you've decided. How about if I call next week? Will you be around on Thursday?"

• "If you like, I can ask Martin to phone you. He's served on the board for years and can give another perspective on our programs."

Keep the ball in your court. Make sure you're the one who's responsible for following up and confirming the decision – yes or no. Then be sure to follow through.

27

The Installment Plan

If you've ever watched late night television – if you've ever watched television, period – you know about the installment plan. "For only $49.99 a month," intones the announcer, "you can own this revolutionary treadmill/kitchen appliance/yard tractor/entertainment center."

People can always give you more money over time than they can give you today. Five hundred dollars may sound like a lot of money, but $40 per month is pretty manageable. Indeed, many families pay more than that for a restaurant meal or cable television service.

Many years ago, my spouse and I were approached for a capital campaign gift of $5,000, which was more money than we had in the bank. It was by far the largest charitable donation we had ever contemplated.

As former staff members of this organization, we were deeply committed to the work. So we suggested installments and made quarterly payments of $250 over five years. Given enough time to factor the contribution into our household budget, we were able to make a really big commitment ... which we fulfilled on schedule.

As a charitable solicitor, the installment plan is your friend. You can incorporate it into your pitch or, if a prospect balks at the size of your request, you can use installments in your fall-back offer:

"I agree, $1,000 is a lot of money. If it would make it more affordable, we can set up monthly or quarterly payments. We like that approach ourselves because it spreads our income throughout the year."

To state the obvious, don't offer the installment plan until you have the infrastructure to back it up. Collection options include:

• Reminder envelopes (old-fashioned and time consuming, but very personal when you add a note)

• Credit card payments

• Electronic fund transfer (or EFT), which is commonly used with monthly donors.

A nice way to suggest an installment gift is to make one yourself and share that information with your prospect. As an added benefit, installments might make it possible for you to increase your contribution, too.

28

Closing: Clarify Your Commitments

Congratulations! You made it through the meeting. You've successfully:

• Presented the work of your organization

• Built a stronger relationship with your prospect by learning about his or her interests and motivations

• Asked for the gift – and received a yes.

One more task remains to be done. It's time to close the meeting.

In the language of sales, "closing" means getting a commitment. You've already done that. Now you need to take the next step – restating any commitments to ensure that everyone leaves the room knowing who's responsible for what.

For example, you might say, "Jessie, thanks again for taking the time to meet, and thanks especially for your pledge. Just so we're both clear about what happens next, I want to review my notes.

"You've agreed to make a gift of $1,000 this year and you're going to pay four quarterly installments of $250 each. That's your responsibility. When I get back to the office, I'll write you a very nice thank you note and enclose an envelope for your first check. Once every three months, I will send you another envelope for your quarterly payment, along with a reminder note. That's my responsibility.

"Am I remembering this correctly?"

"Yes," says the donor, "that's exactly what we agreed to."

Here's another example. "Francesca, before I leave, let me make I sure I know what happens next. As you requested, I'm leaving you materials about our group. You're going to look these over and discuss it with your partner before you decide on your gift. It's my job to call next week to see if you have any other questions, and at that point you'll let me know what you want to do. Am I getting this right?"

I can't overemphasize the importance of clarifying expectations. Far too often, solicitors leave these meetings without clear commitments. Even if the donor isn't ready to say yes or no, negotiate a next step and re-state it clearly.

29

Act IV:
After the Meeting

As you've probably figured out by now, the face to face request is just one phase in a long relationship. The old cliché rings true: up to now you've been courting the prospect, but once the commitment is made – a mutual commitment – it's a lot like marriage, with a different set of joys and responsibilities.

Consider this: *As much as 80 percent of the work in fundraising comes after you receive the gift.* It involves thanking your donors, keeping them informed about the work, and inviting them to participate.

You'll want to set aside time to interact with your contributors in ways that have nothing to do with fundraising. If every contact is about money, sooner or later they will start to feel like ATM machines.

Here's a simple way to make people feel like people. Divide your top tier of donors among the board, so that everyone has a reasonable number of assignments – say, three phone calls per month. If you're assigned people you know, so much the better, but it's not required. The phone call goes something like this:

"Hi, I'm a volunteer board member with (name your group). I'm not calling tonight to ask for money. (Pause for a second and listen to the person gasp in amazement.) I'm just calling to thank you for your support. It means a lot to us.

"Do you have any questions about our work? Do have any interest in being more involved? Is there anything we can do to serve you better?"

For many board members, these phone calls are a revelation. Sure, some people will hang up, but by opening with the words "volunteer board member" you tend to disarm concerns about telemarketers. Many donors will be grateful for the attention; some will give you feedback.

In fact, you can use these calls to conduct an informal member survey: "As you know, we're involved in three program areas. (Describe each in one sentence). Which of these programs are most important to you? Why?"

If you end up talking to an answering machine, you can still transmit the same message: we value your support and we think of you as part of the family.

Phone calls are just one way to reach out to your best donors. Many groups organize recognition events, while others meet with contributors throughout the year. The bottom line is this: if you don't have the time, commitment, and infrastructure to stay in touch with supporters, you shouldn't be soliciting them in the first place. *Before* you launch a fundraising campaign, budget the resources needed to treat donors the way they deserve to be treated.

30

The Most Meaningful Thanks

Have you ever been thanked in a meaningful way? Not simply in response to a charitable gift, but thanked in a memorable way for anything you did? Here's an example of what I mean.

On Veterans Day and Memorial Day, my father goes to local elementary schools to speak about his experiences in World War II. He's a good storyteller and has lots of pictures, so he readily engages the kids.

Once the presentation is over and he leaves, the teacher will hand out markers and say, "Please write a thank you note to Mr. Robinson." Many kids draw pictures of explosions – after all, these are ten-year olds listening to war stories – but some are surprisingly thoughtful.

One student wrote, "I never knew my grandfather, but I knew he was in the war, and now I have a way to think about him." Another wrote, "Mr. Robinson, you da' bomb!" (Translation: you're way cool.)

Obviously, my father is both moved and tickled by these notes. They reinforce his desire to go back into the schools and do it again next year. If you can build a similar "bridge of thanks" between the people who benefit from your work and those who pay for it, imagine the impact.

Other acknowledgement options include personal notes, face-to-face thanks, listing contributor names in your newsletter, purchasing newspaper ads to thank supporters, commemorative items, flowers, food, and donor recognition events. You don't have to overwhelm your donors with thanks, but you must reach out to everyone.

Even board members who shy away from fundraising have a crucial role to play in acknowledging donors. In a healthy organization, everyone says thank you.

31

"We Don't Have to Do This All Year?"

The most effective fundraising campaigns are time-limited events, although the length of time depends on the goal. Capital campaigns, which focus on land or buildings, can run for two or three years. Major universities now have ten-year campaigns, which beg the concept of "time-limited."

Smaller organizations usually lack the infrastructure to sustain multi-year campaigns or even year-round major gifts fundraising. It's certainly possible to set up solicitations throughout the year, but many organizations choose to conduct their major gifts campaign in one concentrated burst over a 10- to 12-week period. This approach offers several advantages.

• A sense of urgency based on deadlines negotiated among the participants.

• Organizational focus. During campaign season,

major gifts fundraising becomes the primary mission of board and fundraising staff.

• The opportunity to recruit and simultaneously train a team of solicitors who can compare notes and learn from each other throughout the process.

• Time off when the asking is over.

Many board members complain about the perpetual pressure to raise money. As an alternative, I suggest you focus board efforts on a time-limited major gifts campaign *because it generates the most money raised per hour of volunteer time.* In the ideal world, this should be the board's primary fundraising activity, period.

If trustees choose to participate in other activities during the rest of the year – organizing house parties, helping with grant proposals, asking friends and family to make donations in lieu of holiday gifts – that's terrific. And if individual board members choose to skip fundraising for the remainder of the year, I can live with that, *as long as they participate fully in the campaign.* During campaign season, everyone's primary commitment is to help with major gifts.

When scheduling your campaign, consider the following questions.

• When are your prospects available?

• When are your solicitors available?

• When are other organizational resources available?

The traditional campaign is led by a volunteer chair or co-chairs who supervise and support three or four team leaders, who in turn supervise and support three or four solicitors each. Make sure that everyone checks in periodically throughout the campaign to compare notes, stay on task, and share success stories.

When it ends, tally up your results and throw yourselves a party to celebrate the effort. Then take some time off – you deserve it!

32

In Praise of Amateurs

Once upon the time, *amateur*s were people who pursued their passions in their spare time for the sheer love of it. Many amateurs – athletes, inventors, naturalists, musicians – were renowned for their expertise, regardless of the fact that they received no pay.

More recently, the word has taken on a slightly negative tone. Yes, amateurs can still be inspired laypersons, but they can also be considered disorganized and incompetent, in the sense of *amateurish.*

I come before you today to sing the praises of amateurs like you. When it comes to asking for money, many volunteers have the unfortunate tendency to defer to the professionals. As stated throughout this book, I believe that volunteers, especially board members, make the best fundraisers. Here are three additional reasons why.

1) Self-interest ... what self-interest? There's no shame raising money for your own salary – I did it for years at several nonprofits – but volunteers have a bit of an advantage: not even a whiff of personal economic benefit. After all, in your capacity as a board member, you receive many rewards, but money is not one of them. Your honored status as a volunteer gives you a lot of credibility.

2) You can ask for help. For amateurs, vulnerability can be a distinct plus. When setting up donor visits by phone, I encourage novices to consider the following appeal.

"Simon, I'm on the board of _____ and one of my responsibilities is to raise money from my friends. It's a bit intimidating, so I'm looking for help. Can I come to your home and practice? It's a real request – I hope you'll consider a gift – but even more than your money, I need your feedback. Maybe you could critique my pitch and help me to make it stronger."

This approach reduces the pressure, because nobody expects a polished presentation. Furthermore, it expands the development team, turning each prospect into an informal fundraising strategist. Finally, it's likely to result in a gift. Who can resist an appeal like that?

It would be hard for a paid professional to use this strategy effectively, but for volunteers, it's almost foolproof.

3) Donors will admire your courage. We tend to think highly of people who test their own limits. When someone does something courageous, we say, "Wow, that was gutsy." While it's hard to put fundraising in the same category as skydiving or mountain climbing, everyone knows that asking for contributions entails some risk...especially when you're doing it as a volunteer. Donors are smart people, and they will respect your commitment.

•••

Given the nature of the world, professional fundraisers will be with us for the long haul, which is a good thing. In addition to managing the fundraising program and dealing with its logistical complexities, a development director's highest calling is to train, support, and facilitate the work of volunteers. But for all the reasons outlined above, professionals should never (and probably will never) take the place of volunteers – and that's a good thing, too.

Believe it or not, your organization can not succeed without your help. You are the ingredient that makes the whole thing work.

33

"Thank You for Asking Me."

A few years ago, I threw myself a party to celebrate 20 years of raising money for social change. As a colleague points out, the world has yet to see a five-year-old who says, "Mommy, when I grow up I want to be a fundraiser." When someone embraces this work for two decades while maintaining a sense of justice and a sense of humor, it is cause for celebration.

Yes, it's a bit odd to throw a party for yourself – I'm grateful to my insistent wife for encouraging me to do it – so in keeping with the theme, we decided to make it a fundraising party. I chose two of my favorite organizations – I was serving on the board of one of them – and designated them as the beneficiaries of the event.

We mailed a very gentle invitation: Donate if you can, but if you can't, please come to the party anyway. It's a potluck so bring food, but if you don't cook, please join us anyway. Please RSVP, but if you decide at the last minute to attend, come on over.

We hired a band, danced all evening, sang songs, ate good food, told stories, laughed a lot, and had the house cleaned up by midnight (which happens when you reach a certain age). We also raised more than $2,000, but that's not the point of this story.

I had mailed invitations to friends across the country, knowing that most would be unable to attend but wanting to let them know about it anyway. One of my friends is an elderly woman, the parent of a former housemate, whom I have known for years. I agonized a bit before inviting her, thinking, "I doubt she can travel. She's probably on a fixed income – can she afford the donation? Am I imposing?" In the end, I decided to send her an invitation because I wanted to honor everything I've been saying in this book.

She responded with a check and a lovely note that said, "Congratulations. It sounds like a fine time. I'm so sorry I won't be able to join you."

And then she wrote something I will never forget: "Thank you for asking me."

When we're raising money, it's easy to feel we're somehow imposing on people, making them uncomfortable, putting them in an awkward position. We forget that all of us are linked together – our shared passions, our common belief in the power of change, is what makes us a community. When we reach out through our organizations, when we encourage people to participate, *we are the ones giving the gift.*

"Thank you for asking me," she said.

It is a privilege to ask. It is also a privilege to be asked. Remember this and you'll be a great fundraiser.

APPENDIX

Appendix A - Sample Gift Pyramid

This chart shows the status of the major gifts campaign about halfway through the solicitations.

Goal: $100,000

GIFTS NEEDED	GIFTS IN HAND	GIFT AMOUNT	CATEGORY TOTAL	TOTAL
1	■ *F. Smith*	$10,000	$10,000	$10,000
3	■ ■ □ *C. Goldstein; D. Lee*	$5,000	$15,000	$25,000
7	□ □ □ □ □ □ □	$2,500	$17,500	$42,500
12	■ ■ ■ ■ ■ □ □ □ □ □ □ □ *M. Cook; R. Rodriguez;* *A. Bielecki; R. Robinson;* *Anonymous*	$1,500	$18,000	$60,500
22	■ ■ ■ ■ □ □ □ □ □ □ □ □ □ □ □ □ □ □ □ □ □ □ *M. Fischer; R. Waterman;* *L. Jones; S. Nguyen*	$1,000	$22,000	$82,500
35	■ □ □ □ □ □ □ □ □ □ □ □ □ □ □ *P. Patel; J. Hermann; M. Smith; J. Farnham* *F. Murphy; K. Saenz; P. Newman; F. Gold;* *J. Davenport; S. Sanjay; R. Muhammed;* *D. Cohen; J. Miller; F. Yamamoto; C. Hickock* *R. Schmook; O. Bean; K. Lieu; K. Delmarva;* *Anonymous (2)*	$500	$17,500	**$100,000**

Adapted from Toxics Action Center.
Names have been changed. Used with permission.

THE AUTHOR

Andy Robinson has been raising money for social change since 1980. As a trainer and consultant, he has assisted nonprofits in 40 states and Canada, leading workshops on fundraising, grantseeking, board development, strategic planning, marketing, leadership development, and earned income strategies.

He specializes in the needs of organizations promoting human rights, social justice, and environmental conservation. In addition to hundreds of local and regional groups, his clients include the American Friends Service Committee, National Wildlife Federation, Neighborhood Reinvestment, National Trust for Historic Preservation, the Evangelical Lutheran Church in America, and the New England Grassroots Environment Fund, where he served as training and outreach director.

Andy is a columnist for *Contributions* and a regular contributor to the *Grassroots Fundraising Journal.* His other books include *Grassroots Grants: An Activist's Guide to Grantseeking* and *Selling Social Change (Without Selling Out): Earned Income Strategies for Nonprofits.* You can reach him at andyfund@earthlink.net.

Raising $1,000 Gifts by Mail Mal Warwick, 112 pp. $24.95.

Whoever heard of raising $1,000 gifts (not to mention $3,000, $4,000, and $5,000 gifts) by mail? That's the realm of personal solicitation, right? Not exclusively, says Mal Warwick. Are you skeptical? Consider just one mailing. A total of 2,352 pieces were mailed to donors who had given $100 or more. This small mailing generated $148,000. Even more impressive, the mailing garnered 54 gifts that topped $1,000!

Raising More Money with Newsletters Than You Ever Thought Possible Tom Ahern, 128 pp., $24.95.

Today, countless organizations are raising more money with their newsletter than with traditional mail appeals. And after reading Tom Ahern's riveting book, it's easy to understand why. Great newsletters have much more going for them. The essence of *Raising More Money with Newsletters Than You Ever Thought Possible* centers around seven fatal flaws. Eliminate them and your newsletter can become a powerful money raiser.

Raising Thousands (if Not Tens of Thousands) of Dollars with Email Madeline Stanionis, 120 pp., $24.95.

At heart, raising money with email is all about building your list, using timing to your advantage, crafting a series of coherent messages, presenting your email in a visually appealing way, and carefully observing your returns for clues to guide your future efforts. Do this as Stanionis advises and you don't have to be the American Red Cross or the Salvation Army to raise a hefty amount of money.

Raising Money Through Bequests
David Valinsky & Melanie Boyd, 105 pp., $24.95.

Members of the "Greatest Generation" are in their 80s and 90s, and as they pass away they're collectively leaving billions of dollars to charitable organizations throughout the U.S. And their preferred vehicle for giving is the simple bequest. If at this very moment you're not marketing your bequest program with G force, you're missing what many are calling the greatest opportunity in the history of fundraising.

The Relentlessly Practical Guide
to Raising Serious Money

Proven Strategies for Nonprofit Organizations
By David Lansdowne, 237 pp., ISBN 1889102199

Why of all the hundreds of fundraising books available did AmeriCorps Vista, with offices throughout the U.S., single this one out as the best and provide a copy to thousands of its staff? Why do colleges and universities throughout the land choose it for their courses?

Why do even fundraising consultants refer back to the book time and again?

Read *Relentless* and you'll quickly understand why.

David Lansdowne plumbs *every* major aspect of fundraising: from annual campaigns to capital campaigns, from major gifts to Internet fundraising, from planned giving to direct mail to prospect research.

Each chapter is delivered with heat-seeking precision. For example, do you want to know how to establish a gift club? Turn to that chapter and chances are you'll learn more in the nine pages than you would from reading an entire book on the subject.

Ditto for writing a case statement. Others have written entire books on the subject, but if you want "just the facts, ma'am" – Lansdowne gives them to you in eight illuminating pages. You won't know every hairsplitting point, but you will be able to produce a creditable case statement after reading what Lansdowne has to say.

There are other standout chapters that lift this book above others.

"The 16 Best Pieces of Fundraising Advice" may be the best rendering of its kind put to pen.

"Fundraising's 20 Biggest Mistakes" is a masterful discussion that alerts you to each and every red flag.

And, "What Every Board Member Must Know to Succeed," should be required reading for any trustee serving a gift-supported organization.

Emerson & Church, Publishers
www.emersonandchurch.com

The Fundraising Habits of
Supremely Successful Boards

A 59-Minute Guide to Assuring Your Organization's Future
By Jerold Panas, 108 pp., ISBN 1889102261

"A large part of virtue consists in good habits," said William Paley.

In his classic book, *The Fundraising Habits of Supremely Successful Boards*, Jerold Panas would rephrase that a bit: A large part of an organization's success depends on its board's willingness to cultivate certain behaviors.

Over the course of a storied career, Panas has worked with literally thousands of boards. He has counseled foundering groups; he's been the wind beneath the wings of boards whose organizations have soared.

In fact, it's a safe bet that Panas has observed more boards at work than perhaps anyone in America, all the while helping them to surpass campaign goals of $100,000 to $100 million.

Funnel every ounce of that experience into a single book and what you have is *The Fundraising Habits*, the brilliant culmination of what Panas has learned firsthand about boards who excel at the task of resource development.

Anyone who has read *Asking* or any of Panas' other books knows his style – an irresistible mix of storytelling, exhortation, and inspiration.

Habits follows the same engaging mold, offering a panoply of habits any board would be wise to cultivate. Some are specific, with measurable outcomes. Others are more intangible, with Panas seeking to impart an attitude of success.

In all, there are 25 habits and each is explored in two- and three-page chapters ... and all of them animated by engaging anecdotes and real-life stories that only this grandmaster of philanthropy can tell.

Emerson & Church, Publishers
www.emersonandchurch.com

Copies of this and other books
by the publisher are available at discount
when purchased in quantity for boards of
directors or staff. Call 508-359-0019 or visit
www.emersonandchurch.com.

Emerson
& Church
PUBLISHERS